ON HUMAN LIFE
HUMANAE VITAE

D0982284

ON HUMAN LIFE

HUMANAE VITAE

Pope Paul VI

Foreword by Mary Eberstadt
Afterword by James Hitchcock
Postscript by Jennifer Fulwiler

IGNATIUS PRESS   SAN FRANCISCO

Cover design by Roxanne Mei Lum

© 2014 by Ignatius Press, San Francisco
All rights reserved
ISBN 978-1-62164-001-1
Library of Congress Control Number 2014949935
Printed in the United States of America ∞

CONTENTS

Foreword: The Vindication of *Humanae Vitae*,
   by Mary Eberstadt 7

HUMANAE VITAE 45

A Historical Afterword,
   by James Hitchcock 87

Postscript: We're Finally Ready for *Humanae
   Vitae*, by Jennifer Fulwiler 103

For Further Reading 109

FOREWORD

The Vindication of *Humanae Vitae*

by Mary Eberstadt

Of all the paradoxical fallout from the Pill, perhaps the least understood today is this: the most unfashionable, unwanted, and ubiquitously deplored moral teaching on earth is also the most thoroughly vindicated by the accumulation of secular, empirical, post-revolutionary fact.

The document in question is of course *Humanae Vitae*, the encyclical letter of Pope Paul VI on the subject of the regulation of birth, published on July 25, 1968. Now, that *Humanae Vitae* and related Catholic teachings about sexual morality are laughingstocks in all the best places is not exactly news. Even among believers, everybody grasps that this is one doctrine the world loves to hate. Routine secular reporting on the Church rarely fails to mention the teachings of *Humanae Vitae,* usually alongside adjectives like "divisive" and "controversial" and "outdated". In fact, if there's anything on earth that unites the Church's adversaries, the teaching against contraception is probably it.

To many people, both today and when the encyclical was promulgated, the notion simply defies understanding. Consenting adults, told not to use birth control? Preposterous. Third World parents deprived access to contraception and abortion? Positively criminal. A ban on condoms when there's a risk of contracting AIDS? Beneath contempt. "The execration of the world", in philosopher G. E. M. Anscombe's phrase, was what Paul VI incurred with that document—to which the years since 1968 have added plenty of just plain ridicule.[1] Hasn't everyone heard Monty Python's send-up song "Every Sperm Is Sacred"? Or heard the jokes? "You no play-a the game, you no make-a the rules." And "What do

---

[1] G. E. M. Anscombe, *Contraception and Chastity* (London: Catholic Truth Society, 1975), reprinted in Janet E. Smith, ed., *Why* Humanae Vitae *Was Right: A Reader* (San Francisco: Ignatius Press, 1993), pp. 121–46.

you call the rhythm method? *Vatican roulette.*" And "What do you call a woman who uses the rhythm method? *Mommy.*"

As everyone also knows, it's not only the Church's self-declared adversaries who go in for this sort of sport—so, too, do many American and European Catholics. *I may be Catholic, but I'm not a maniac about it,* runs their unofficial subtext —meaning, *I'm happy to take credit for enlightened Catholic positions on the death penalty, social justice, and civil rights, but, of course, I don't believe in those archaic teachings about divorce, sexuality, and, above all, birth control.*

Such is the current fate of *Humanae Vitae* and all it represents in the Church in America— and, for that matter, in what is left of the advanced Western one, too. With each passing year, it seems safe to assume, fewer priests can be found to explain the teaching, fewer parishioners to obey it, and fewer educated people to avoid rolling their eyes at the idea that anyone by now could possibly be so antiquarian or purposefully perverse as to hold any opinion about contraceptive sex—any, that is, other than its full-throttle celebration as the chief liberation of our time.

And in just that apparent consensus about the ridiculousness of it all, amid all those ashes scattered over a Christian teaching stretching back two millennia, arises a fascinating and in fact exceedingly amusing modern morality tale —amusing, at least, to those who take their humor dark.

"He who sits in the heavens laughs" (Ps 2:4), the Psalmist promises, specifically in a passage about enjoying vindication over one's adversaries. If that is so, then the racket by now must be prodigious. Not only have the document's signature predictions been ratified in empirical force, but they have been ratified as few predictions ever are: in ways its authors could not possibly have foreseen, including by information that did not exist when the document was written, by scholars and others with no interest whatever in its teaching, and indeed even inadvertently, and in more ways than one, by many proud public adversaries of the Church.

Forty-plus years after *Humanae Vitae*, fifty-plus after the approval of the Pill, there are more than enough ironies, both secular and religious, to make one swear there's a humorist in heaven.

Begin by meditating upon what might be called the first of the secular ironies now evident: *Humanae Vitae*'s specific predictions about what the world would look like if artificial contraception became widespread. The encyclical warned of four resulting trends: a general lowering of moral standards throughout society; a rise in infidelity; a lessening of respect for women by men; and the coercive use of reproductive technologies by governments.

In the years since *Humanae Vitae*'s appearance, numerous distinguished Catholic thinkers have argued, using a variety of evidence, that each of these predictions has been borne out by the social facts. One thinks, for example, of Monsignor George A. Kelly in his 1978 "The Bitter Pill the Catholic Community Swallowed" and of the many contributions of Janet E. Smith, including Humanae Vitae: *A Generation Later* and the edited volume *Why* Humanae Vitae *Was Right: A Reader.*[2]

---

[2] Monsignor George A. Kelly, "The Bitter Pill the Catholic Community Swallowed", collected in *The Battle for the Catholic Mind: Catholic Faith and Catholic Intellect in the Work of the Fellowship of Catholic Scholars, 1978–95,* ed. William E. May and Kenneth D. Whitehead (South Bend, Ind.: St. Augustine's Press, 2001, published in association with the Fellowship

And therein lies an irony within an irony. Although it is largely *Catholic* thinkers who have connected the latest empirical evidence to the defense of *Humanae Vitae*'s predictions, during those same years many of the experts actually *producing* the empirical evidence have been secular social scientists. As sociologist W. Bradford Wilcox put it a decade ago, "The leading scholars who have tackled these topics are not Christians, and most of them are not political or social conservatives. They are, rather, honest social scientists willing to follow the data wherever it may lead."[3]

Consider Nobel Prize-winning economist George Akerlof. In a well-known 1996 article in the *Quarterly Journal of Economics*, Akerlof explained, using the language of modern economics, why the sexual revolution—contrary to common prediction, especially prediction by those in and out of the Church who wanted the

---

of Catholic Scholars), pp. 41–109. See also Janet E. Smith, Humanae Vitae: *A Generation Later* (Washington, D.C.: Catholic University of America Press, 1991), and *Why* Humanae Vitae *Was Right* referenced above.

[3] W. Bradford Wilcox, "The Facts of Life and Marriage: Social Science and the Vindication of Christian Moral Teaching", *Touchstone*, January—February, 2005, www.touchstone mag.com/archives/article.php?id=18-01-038-f

teaching on birth control changed—had led to an increase in both illegitimacy and abortion.[4] In another work published in the *Economic Journal* in 1998, he traced the empirical connections between the decrease in marriage and married fatherhood for men—both clear consequences of the contraceptive revolution—and the simultaneous increase in behaviors to which single men appear more prone: substance abuse, incarceration, and arrests, to name just three.[5]

He explained his findings in nontechnical terms in *Slate* magazine: "Although doubt will always remain about what causes a change in social custom, the technology-shock theory does fit the facts. The new reproductive technology was adopted quickly, and on a massive scale. Marital and fertility patterns changed with similar drama, at about the same time."[6]

To these examples of secular social science

---

[4] George A. Akerlof, Janet L. Yellen, and Michael L. Katz, "An Analysis of Out-of-Wedlock Childbearing in the United States", *Quarterly Journal of Economics* 111, no. 2 (1996): 277–317.
[5] George A. Akerlof, "Men Without Children", *Economic Journal* 108 (1998): 287–309.
[6] George A. Akerlof and Janet L. Yellen, "Why Kids Have Kids", November 16, 1996, http://www.slate.com/articles/briefing/articles/1996/11/why_kids_have_kids.html

confirming what Catholic thinkers had predicted, one might add many more demonstrating the negative effects on children and society. The groundbreaking work that Daniel Patrick Moynihan did in 1965, on the black family, is an example, as is the research of Judith Wallerstein, Barbara Dafoe Whitehead, Sara McLanahan, Gary Sandefur, and David Blankenhorn, among other scholars. More landmark works on the benefits of marriage and the downside of its decline include James Q. Wilson's *The Marriage Problem*, Linda Waite and Maggie Gallagher's *The Case for Marriage*, Kay Hymowitz's *Marriage and Caste in America*, and Elizabeth Marquardt's *Between Two Worlds: The Inner Lives of Children of Divorce*. All support the proposition that the sexual revolution has been resulting in disaster for large swaths of society—a proposition further honed by decades of examination of the relation between public welfare and family dysfunction (particularly in the pages of the decidedly not-Catholic *Public Interest* magazine). Post-revolutionary sexual habits have been having massive public consequences, as noted among other places in Charles Murray's seminal 1984 study of welfare policy, *Losing Ground*; and in

Francis Fukuyama's 1999 book, *The Great Disruption: Human Nature and the Reconstitution of Social Order.*[7]

All this is to say that, beginning just before the appearance of *Humanae Vitae*, an academic and intellectual rethinking began that can no longer be ignored—one whose accumulation of empirical evidence points to the deleterious effects of the sexual revolution on many adults and children.

Some secular scholars now further link these problems to the contraceptive revolution itself. Consider the work of maverick sociobiologist Lionel Tiger. Hardly a cat's-paw of the pope—he describes religion as "a toxic issue"—Tiger has repeatedly emphasized the centrality of the sexual revolution to today's unique problems. *The Decline of Males*, his 1999 book, was particularly controversial among feminists for its argument that female contraceptives had altered the balance

---

[7] Charles Murray, *Losing Ground: American Social Policy, 1950–1980* (New York: Basic Books, 1984); Francis Fukuyama, *The Great Disruption: Human Nature and the Reconstitution of Social Order* (New York: Free Press, 1999). Fukuyama called the Pill one of the two most influential features of the age, the other being the shift in labor from a manufacturing to an information-based economy.

between the sexes in disturbing new ways (especially by taking from men any say in whether they could have children).[8]

Equally eyebrow-raising, at least in secular circles, is his linking of contraception to the breakdown of families, female impoverishment, trouble in the relationship between the sexes, and single motherhood. Tiger has further argued—as *Humanae Vitae* did not explicitly—that "contraception causes abortion".[9]

Who could deny that the predictions of *Humanae Vitae* and, by extension, of Catholic moral theology have been ratified with data and arguments that did not even exist in 1968? But now comes the question that just keeps on giving. Has this dramatic reappraisal of the empirically known universe led to any wider secular reappraisals, however grudging, that the Catholic Church may have gotten something right after all? The answer is manifestly that it has not. And this is only the beginning of the dissonance that surrounds us.

---

[8] Lionel Tiger, *The Decline of Males: The First Look at an Unexpected New World for Men and Women* (Darby, Pa.: Diane Publishing, 1999), p. 20.

[9] Ibid., p. 27.

The years since the Pill's approval have similarly destroyed the mantle called "science" that *Humanae Vitae*'s detractors once wrapped around themselves. In particular, the doomsday population science so popular and influential during the era in which *Humanae Vitae* appeared has been repeatedly demolished.

Born from Thomas Robert Malthus' famous late-eighteenth-century *Essay on Population*, this was the novel view that humanity itself amounted to a kind of scourge or pollution whose pressure on fellow members would lead to catastrophe. Though rooted in other times and places, Malthusianism of one particular variety was fully in bloom in America by the early 1960s. In fact, *Humanae Vitae* appeared two months before the most successful popularization of Malthusian thinking yet: Paul R. Ehrlich's *The Population Bomb*, which opened with the ominous words: "The battle to feed all of humanity is over. In the 1970s and 1980s hundreds of millions of people will starve to death in spite of any crash programs embarked upon now."[10]

---

[10] Paul Ehrlich, *The Population Bomb: Population Control or Race to Oblivion?* (New York: Sierra Club—Ballantine Books, 1970), p. xi.

If, as George Weigel has suggested, 1968 was absolutely the worst moment for *Humanae Vitae* to appear, it could not have been a better one for Ehrlich to advance his apocalyptic thesis.[11] An entomologist who specialized in butterflies, Ehrlich found an American public, including a generation of Catholics, extraordinarily receptive to his direst thoughts about humanity.

This was the wave that *The Population Bomb* caught on its way to becoming one of the best-sellers of its time. Of course, many people with no metaphysics whatsoever were drawn to Ehrlich's doom-mongering. But for restless Catholics, in particular, the overpopulation scare was attractive—for if overpopulation could be posited as the problem, the putative solution was

---

[11] See George Weigel, *Witness to Hope: The Biography of Pope John Paul II* (New York: HarperCollins, 1999), p. 210: "The timing of *Humanae Vitae*", he writes, "could not have been worse; 1968, a year of revolutionary enthusiasms, was not the moment for calm, measured reflection on anything. It is doubtful whether any reiteration of the classic Catholic position on marital chastity, no matter how persuasively argued, could have been heard in such circumstances. On the other hand, one has to ask why a position that defended 'natural' means of fertility regulation was deemed impossibly antiquarian at precisely the moment when 'natural' was becoming one of the sacred words in the developed world, especially with regard to ecological consciousness."

obvious: Make the Church lift the ban on birth control.

It is less than coincidental that the high-mindedness of saving the planet dovetailed perfectly with a more self-interested outcome: the freer pursuit of sexuality via the Pill. Dissenting Catholics had special reasons to stress the "science of overpopulation", and so they did. In the name of a higher morality, their argument went, birth control could be defended as the lesser of two evils (a position argued by the dissenter Charles Curran, among others).

Less than half a century later, these preoccupations with overwhelming birth rates appear practically as pseudoscientific as phrenology. Actually, that may be unfair to phrenology. For the overpopulation literature has not only been abandoned by thinkers for more improved science; it has been so thoroughly proved false that today's cutting-edge theory worries about precisely the opposite: a "birth dearth" that is "graying" the advanced world. By 2008, Columbia University historian Matthew Connelly could publish *Fatal Misconception: The Struggle to Control World Population* and garner a starred review in *Publishers Weekly*—the single best contemporary demolition of the population arguments that some once hoped would undermine Church teaching.[12] This is all the more satisfying a ratification because Connelly is so conscientious in establishing his own personal antagonism toward the Catholic Church (at one point asserting without even a footnote that natural family planning "still fails most couples who try it").

Population "science" was not only failing to help people, Connelly argues, but also actively harming some of them—and in a way that summoned some of the baser episodes of recent historical memory:

> The great tragedy of population control, the fatal misconception, was to think that one could know other people's interests better than they knew it themselves. . . . The essence of population control, whether it targeted migrants, the "unfit", or families that seemed either too big or too small, was to make rules for other people without having to answer to them. . . . [O]pponents were essentially correct in viewing it as another chapter in the unfinished business of imperialism.[13]

---

[12] Matthew Connelly, *Fatal Misconception: The Struggle to Control World Population* (Cambridge, Mass.: Belknap Press, 2008).
[13] Ibid., p. 378.

As a related matter, the years since *Humanae Vitae* appeared have also vindicated the encyclical's fear that governments would use the new contraceptive technology coercively. The outstanding example, of course, is the Chinese government's long-running "one-child policy", replete with forced abortions, public tracking of menstrual cycles, family flight, increased female infanticide, sterilization, and other assaults too numerous even to begin cataloguing here. Lesser-known examples include the Indian government's foray into coercive use of contraception in the "emergency" of 1976 and 1977, and the Indonesian government's practice in the 1970s and 1980s of the bullying implantation of IUDs and Norplant.

"Who will prevent rulers", warns *Humanae Vitae* (no. 17), "from favoring, and even imposing upon their people, the method of contraception they judge to be the most effective, if they should consider this to be necessary?" As with the unintended affirmation by social science, will anyone within the ranks of the population revisionists now give credit where credit is due?

Perhaps the most mocked of *Humanae Vitae*'s predictions was its claim that separating sex from procreation would deform relations between the sexes and consequently a "wide and easy road would thus be opened to conjugal infidelity and to a general lowering of morality" (no. 17). In a day when advertisements exploiting sex scream from almost every billboard and webpage and when almost every Western family has its share as never before of broken homes and divorce and abortion, most might wonder what further proof could possibly be needed.

But just to leave matters there would be to miss something important. The critical point is, one might say, not so much the proof as the pudding it's in. And it would be hard to get more ironic than having these particular predictions of *Humanae Vitae* vindicated by perhaps the most unlikely—to say nothing of unwilling—witness of all: modern feminism.

Yet that is exactly what has happened since 1968. From Betty Friedan and Gloria Steinem to Andrea Dworkin and Germaine Greer on up through Susan Faludi and Naomi Wolf, feminist literature has been a remarkably consistent and uninterrupted cacophony of grievance, recrimination, and sexual discontent. In that record—written by the revolution's very defenders—we find, as nowhere else, personal testimony of what the revolution has done to womankind. Paradoxically, the liberation of women from the supposed chains of reproduction does not appear to have made womankind happier. In fact, to judge by popular literature, it has made them unhappier than ever—a point that has also been made astutely by a number of contrary-minded social observers including Midge Decter, Danielle Crittenden, and F. Carolyn Graglia.[14]

Just read their books. If feminists married and had children, they lamented it. If they failed to marry or have children, they lamented that, too. If they worked outside the home and also tended their children, they complained about how hard that was. If they worked outside the

---

[14] See, among her many other trenchant critiques of feminism, Midge Decter, *An Old Wife's Tale: My Seven Decades in Love and War* (New York: William Morrow, 2001). See also Danielle Crittenden, *What Our Mothers Didn't Tell Us: Why Happiness Eludes the Modern Woman* (New York: Simon and Schuster, 1999), and F. Carolyn Graglia, *Domestic Tranquility: A Brief against Feminism* (Dallas, Tex.: Spence, 1998).

home and didn't tend their children, they ex-
coriated anyone who thought they should. And
running through all this literature is a more or
less constant invective about the unreliability and
disrespect of men.

The signature metaphors of feminism say everything we need to know about how happy liberation has been making these women: the subur-
ban home as concentration camp, men as rapists,
children as intolerable burdens, fetuses as para-
sites, and so on. These are the sounds of liberation? Even the vaunted right to abortion, both
claimed and exercised at extraordinary rates, did
not seem to mitigate the misery of millions of
these women after the sexual revolution.

Coming full circle, feminist and *Vanity Fair*
contributor Leslie Bennetts has argued that women need to protect themselves financially and
otherwise from dependence on men, including
from men deserting them later in life. Mothers
cannot afford to stay home with their children,
she says, because they cannot trust their men not
to leave them. Similarly, feminist Linda Hirshman penned a ferocious and widely read mani-
festo almost ten years ago urging, among other

bitter "solutions", that women protect themselves by adopting—in effect—a voluntary one-child policy.[15]

Beneath all the pathos, the subtext remains the same: Woman's chief adversary is Unreliable Man, who does not understand her sexual and romantic needs and who walks off time and again at the first sashay of a younger thing. What are all these but the generic cries of a woman who thinks that men are "disregarding her physical and emotional equilibrium" and "no longer considering her as his partner whom he should surround with care and affection"?[16]

Perhaps the most compelling case made for traditional marriage lately was not on the cover of, say, *Catholic World Report* but in the devoutly secular *Atlantic*. The 2008 article "Marry Him!" by Lori Gottlieb—a single mother who conceived her only child with donor sperm rather than miss out on motherhood as she has on marriage—is a frank and excruciatingly personal look into some

---

[15] Linda Hirshman, "Homeward Bound", *American Prospect*, November 22, 2005.

[16] Pope Paul VI, *Humanae Vitae*, July 25, 1968, 17 [Vatican translation].

of the sexual revolution's lonelier venues, including the creation of children by anonymous or absent sperm donors, the utter corrosiveness of taking a consumerist approach to romance, and the miserable effects of advancing age on one's sexual marketability.[17] As such, it is one among many unwitting testimonials written by women themselves about some of the funny things that happened after the Pill freed everybody once and for all.

That there is no auxiliary literature of grievance for men—who, for the most part, just don't seem to feel they have as much to grieve about in this new world order—is something else that *Humanae Vitae* and a few other retrograde types saw coming in the wake of the revolution. As the saying goes, *cui bono*? Decades later, the evidence is in. As Archbishop Charles J. Chaput observed on *Humanae Vitae*'s thirtieth anniversary in 1998, "Contraception has released males—to a historically unprecedented degree—from responsibil-

---

[17] Lori Gottlieb, "Marry Him!", *Atlantic*, February 2008, http://www.theatlantic.com/magazine/archive/2008/03/marry -him/6651/

ity for their sexual aggression."[18] Will any man or woman who honestly disagrees with that statement please stand up?

The years since *Humanae Vitae* have witnessed one more phenomenon shedding retrospective credit on the Church: a serious reappraisal of Christian sexuality from some leading Protestant thinkers.

Thus, for instance, Albert Mohler, president of the Southern Baptist Theological Seminary, observed in *First Things* over fifteen years ago that "in an ironic turn, American evangelicals are rethinking birth control even as a majority of the nation's Roman Catholics indicate a rejection of their Church's teaching."[19] Later, when interviewed for an article in the New York Times Sunday magazine about current religious

---

[18] Archbishop Charles J. Chaput, 1998 pastoral letter, adapted in "Forty Years Later: Pope's Concern in *Humanae Vitae* Vindicated", *Denver Catholic Register*, July 22, 2008, http://www.archden.org/dcr/news.php?e=480&s=2&a=10086

[19] Quoted in R. Albert Mohler Jr., "Can Christians Use Birth Control?", AlbertMohler.com, May 8, 2006 (originally available March 30, 2004), http://www.albertmohler.com/2006/05/08/can-christians-use-birth-control/

thinking on artificial contraception, Mohler elaborated:

> I cannot imagine any development in human history, after the Fall, that has had a greater impact on human beings than the Pill. . . . The entire horizon of the sexual act changes. I think there can be no question that the Pill gave incredible license to everything from adultery and affairs to premarital sex and within marriage to a separation of the sex act and procreation.[20]

Mohler also observed that this legacy of damage was affecting the younger generation of evangelicals. "I detect a huge shift. Students on our campus are intensely concerned. Not a week goes by that I do not get contacted by pastors about the issue. There are active debates going on. It's one of the things that may serve to divide evangelicalism."[21]

As a corollary to such rethinking, experience seems to have taught a similar lesson to at least some of the Millennials—the generation to grow up under divorce, widespread contraception, fa-

---

[20] Quoted in Russell Shorto, "Contra-Contraception", *New York Times Magazine*, May 7, 2006, http://www.nytimes.com/2006/05/07/magazine/07contraception.html?pagewanted=all
[21] Ibid.

therless households, and all the other emancipatory fallout. As Naomi Schaefer Riley noted in the *Wall Street Journal* several years ago about a 2008 contretemps at Notre Dame, "The students are probably the most religious part of the Notre Dame [University]. . . . Younger Catholics tend to be among the more conservative ones."[22]

Similarly, it is hard to imagine that something like the traditionalist, ecumenical Anscombe Society at Princeton University, started in 2004, could have been founded in 1968—let alone that a movement dedicated to chastity and traditionalism would also come to have satellites on many other campuses via the Love and Fidelity Network. Nor is there any mistaking that at least some of the return to traditionalism is being spurred by this critical fact, poorly understood in the more sophisticated circles of the West: at least some of the initial victims have come to turn on the revolution itself. As evangelical author Joe Carter has put it, in testimony that

---

[22] Naomi Schaefer Riley, "Rev. John I. Jenkins, Catholicism, Inc.", *Wall Street Journal*, April 12, 2008, http://online.wsj.com/article/SB 120796155333509621-search.html?KEYWORDS=Catholicism+Inc+riley&COLLECTION=wsjie/6month

would resonate with many people younger than
the Boomers:

> Having grown up either in a broken home or sur-
> rounded by friends who did, we X-Cons [Gen-
> eration X Conservatives] recognize the value of
> traditional family structures. We may not always
> be successful in building permanent relationships
> ourselves, but we value the bonds of family more
> than the previous generation.[23]

A similar force making traditionalists of these
younger Americans, judging by surveys and other
data, is the fact of their having grown up in a
world characterized by abortion on demand. And
this brings us to yet another irony worth contem-
plating: what widespread rejection of *Humanae
Vitae* has done to the character of Catholicism in
America, specifically—what might also be called
the Catholic version of the orphan with chutz-
pah.

Thus many complain about the dearth of priests,
all the while ignoring their own responsibility for
that outcome—the fact that few have children

---

[23] Joe Carter, "X-Cons: The Conservative Mind of Generation X", *First Things*, from the daily column "On the Square",
May 18, 2011, http://www.firstthings.com/onthesquare/2011/
05/x-cons-the-conservative-mind-of-generation-x

in numbers large enough to send one son to the priesthood while others marry and carry on the family name. Some mourn the closing of Catholic churches and schools—never mind that whole parishes, claiming the rights of individual conscience, have contracepted themselves out of existence. Some point to the priest sex scandals as proof positive that chastity is too much to ask of people—completely ignoring that it was the randy absence of chastity that created the scandals in the first place.

In fact, the disgrace of contemporary Catholicism—the scandals involving priests and underage boys—is surely traceable at least in part to the collusion between a Catholic laity that wanted a different birth-control doctrine, on the one hand, and a new generation of priests cutting themselves a different kind of slack, on the other. It is hard to believe that either new development —the widespread open rebellion against Church sexual teachings by the laity, or the concomitant quiet rebellion against Church sexual teachings by a significant number of priests—could have existed without the other.

In sum, one has heard a thousand times the insistence that *Humanae Vitae* somehow sparked a rebellion or was something new under the sun. To the contrary, all that Paul VI did—as philosopher Anscombe among many other unapologetic Catholics then and since have pointed out—was to reiterate what just about everyone authoritative in the history of Christianity had ever said on the subject until practically the day before yesterday.

It was, in a word, no. Only a little over a hundred years ago, for example, the Lambeth Conference of 1908 affirmed its opposition to contraception in words harsher than anything appearing in *Humanae Vitae*: "demoralizing to character and hostile to national welfare".[24] In

---

[24] In addition, three of the 1908 conference's seventy-eight resolutions addressed the subject with a specificity and degree of hostility that would surely come as shocks to most Anglicans today—Resolution 41: "The Conference regards with alarm the growing practice of the artificial restriction of the family, and earnestly calls upon all Christian people to discountenance the use of all artificial means of restriction as demoralising to character and hostile to national welfare." Resolution 42: "The Conference affirms that deliberate tampering with nascent life is repugnant to Christian morality." Resolution 43: "The Conference expresses most cordial appreciation of the services rendered by those medical men who have borne courageous

another historical twist that must have someone laughing somewhere, pronouncements of
the founding fathers of Protestantism make the
Catholic traditionalists of 1968 look positively
diffident. Martin Luther in a commentary on the
Book of Genesis declared contraception to be
worse than incest or adultery. John Calvin called
it an "unforgivable crime".[25] The unanimity of
Christian teaching on the subject was not abandoned until the year 1930, when the Anglicans
voted to allow married couples to use birth control in extreme cases, and one denomination after another over the years came to follow suit.

Seen in the light of actual Christian tradition,
the question is not after all why the Catholic Church refused to concede the point. It is
rather why just about everyone else in the Judeo-

---

testimony against the injurious practices spoken of, and appeals
with confidence to them and to their medical colleagues to
co-operate in creating and maintaining a wholesome public
opinion on behalf of the reverent use of the married state" (*The
Lambeth Conference: Resolutions Archive from 1908*, published by
the Anglican Communion Office, 2005, available online at
http://www.lambethconference.org/resolutions/index.cfm).

[25] Quoted in Charles D. Provan, *The Bible and Birth Control*
(Monongahela, Pa.: Zimmer Printing, 1989), http://www.jes
us-passion.com/contraception.htm

Christian tradition did. Whatever the answer, the Catholic Church took, and continues to take, the public fall for causing a collapse—when actually, in theological and historical terms, she was the only one not collapsing.

From time to time since 1968, some of the Catholics who accepted "the only doctrine that had ever appeared as the teaching of the Church on these things",[26] in Anscombe's words, have puzzled over why, exactly, *Humanae Vitae* has been so poorly received by the rest of the world. Surely part of it is timing, as George Weigel observed. Others have cited an implacably secular media and the absence of a national pulpit for Catholics as contributing factors. Still others have floated the idea that John Paul II's *Theology of the Body*, an elaborate and highly positive explication of Christian moral teaching, might have taken some of the sting out of *Humanae Vitae* and better won the obedience of the flock.

At the end of the day, though, it is hard to believe that the fundamental force behind the ex-

---

[26] Janet E. Smith, *Why Humanae Vitae Was Right: A Reader* (San Francisco: Ignatius Press, 1993), p. 132.

ecration by the world amounts to a phrase here and there in *Humanae Vitae*—or in Augustine, or in Thomas Aquinas, or in the 1930 encyclical *Casti Connubii*, or anywhere else in the long history of Christian teaching on the subject. More likely, the fundamental issue is rather what Archbishop Chaput has explained: "If Paul VI was right about so many of the consequences deriving from contraception, it is because he was right about contraception itself."[27]

This is exactly the connection few people want to make today, because contraceptive sex—as commentators from all over, religious or not, agree—is the fundamental social fact of our time. And the fierce and widespread desire to keep it so is responsible for a great many perverse outcomes. Despite an empirical record that is unmistakably on Paul VI's side by now, there is extraordinary resistance to crediting Catholic moral teaching with having been right about anything, empiricism be damned.

---

[27] Charles J. Chaput, O.F.M. Cap., Archbishop of Denver, "On Human Life: A Pastoral Letter to the People of God of Northern Colorado on the Truth and Meaning of Married Love", July 22, 1998, available online at http://guweb2.gonzaga.edu/~dewolf/chaput.htm

Considering the human spectacle today, decades after the document whose widespread rejection reportedly broke Paul VI's heart, one can't help but wonder how he and his theologians might have felt if they had glimpsed only a fraction of the evidence now available—whether any of it might have provoked just the smallest wry smile.

After all, it would take a heart of stone not to find at least some of what's now out there funny as hell. There is the ongoing empirical vindication in one arena after another of the most unwanted, ignored, and ubiquitously mocked global teaching of the past fifty years. There is the fact that the Pill, which was supposed to erase all consequences of sex once and for all, turned out to have huge consequences of its own. There is the way that so many Catholics, embarrassed by accusations of archaism and driven by their own desires to be as free for sex as everyone around them, went racing for the theological exit signs after *Humanae Vitae*—all this just as the world with its wicked old ways began stockpiling more evidence for the Church's doctrine than anyone living in previous centuries could have imagined, and while still other people were actually being brought closer to the Church because she stood exactly as that "sign of contradiction" when so many in the world wanted otherwise.

Yet instead of vindication for the Church, there is demoralization; instead of clarity, mass confusion; instead of more obedience, ever less. Really, the perversity is, well, perverse. In what other area does humanity operate at this level of extreme, daily, constant contradiction? Where is the Boccaccio for this post-Pill *Decameron*? It really is all very funny, when you stop to think about it. So why isn't everybody down here laughing?

HUMANAE VITAE

Encyclical Letter of
His Holiness Pope Paul VI
On the Regulation of Births

This revised translation of Pope Paul VI's Encyclical Letter, *Humanae Vitae*, was originally prepared by Rev. Marc Calegari, S.J., on the occasion of the symposium of July 1978, sponsored by the Archdiocese of San Francisco and by the Saint Ignatius Institute of the University of San Francisco, to commemorate the tenth anniversary of the Encyclical's promulgation. Fr. Calegari subsequently revised his translation in 1985. Fr. Calegari died in October 1992.

REVISOR'S NOTE

The English and the other vernacular translations of *Humanae Vitae*, along with the Latin text, were released in the Vatican on July 29, 1968. These translations were made from the Italian. Why not from the Latin? Presumably because the Latin was not available when the modern language translators began their work. The Latin translation was being prepared from the Italian at the same time as were the other translations.

A first revision of the Vatican's English translation, made chiefly to eliminate some renderings that seemed too literal, was published in *Catholic Mind* of September 1968.

A second and more extensive revision was published for the Archdiocese of San Francisco/ University of San Francisco celebration of the tenth anniversary of *Humanae Vitae*. The process of revision has continued since 1978.

The revisor's primary concern remains fidelity to the Italian original. It is left to a future translator to bring about a more satisfactory union of elegance and accuracy, perhaps on the occasion of a later anniversary celebration of *Humanae Vitae*.

It should be noted that any attempt to deepen one's understanding of *Humanae Vitae* by a more intensive study of the Latin translation of the encyclical (or of English translations of the Latin translation) is an exercise of limited value, given the origin of the Latin text, the kind of Latin used and the resulting distance from the original.

It is true that the Latin text is the official text, but there are few if any passages in the encyclical where an appeal to the Latin would be needed to resolve a disputed point. However, an asterisk [*] is used on a number of occasions to call attention to some interesting differences between the Italian and the Latin. It is paradoxical and even regrettable, but certainly obvious, that the original text often gives a more accurate reading of the author's mind than does the official text.

Some encyclicals were originally written in Latin, but these have been few. The Vatican itself has from time to time released information about the original language of some encyclicals: for example, *Rerum Novarum* of 1891 (Italian), *Ecclesiam Suam* of 1964 (Italian), *Populorum Progressio* of 1967 (French), *Redemptor Hominis* of 1979 (Polish).

M. A. CALEGARI, S.J.

October, 1985

HUMANAE VITAE

Encyclical Letter of
His Holiness Pope Paul VI
On the Regulation of Births

*To the venerable patriarchs and archbishops, to
the bishops and other local ordinaries in peace
and communion with the Apostolic See, to the
clergy, to the faithful, and to all men of good will.*

Venerable brothers and beloved sons:

The Transmission of Life

1. The very serious duty of transmitting human life, by reason of which husbands and wives are free and responsible collaborators with God the Creator, has always been for them a source of great joys—joys, however, sometimes accompanied by much difficulty and distress.

At all times the fulfillment of this duty has posed serious problems to the conscience of married persons. But with the recent evolution of society, changes have taken place that raise new questions which the Church could not ignore since they had to do with matters touching so closely the life and happiness of men.

I. NEW ASPECTS OF THE PROBLEM AND THE COMPETENCY OF THE MAGISTERIUM

2. The changes that have taken place are, in fact, noteworthy and of various kinds. In the first place, there is rapid population growth, which causes many to fear that world population is increasing more rapidly than available resources, with the consequence of growing distress for so many families and developing countries. Therefore, authorities are greatly tempted to counter this danger with radical measures. Today, moreover, conditions of work and of housing as well as increased demands both in the economic field and in the field of education, often make the adequate support of a large number of children difficult.

There also has been a change in how people consider the person of woman and her place in society. There has been a change, too, in the value attributed to conjugal love in marriage and to the significance of conjugal acts in relation to that love.

Finally, and above all, man has made stupendous progress in the mastery and rational organization of the forces of nature, so that he tends to extend this mastery to his own total being: to the body, to psychic life, to social life and even to the laws that regulate the transmission of life.

3. Such a situation gives rise to new questions. Given the conditions of life today, and given the importance that conjugal relations have for harmony between husband and wife and for their mutual fidelity, would not a revision of the ethical norms in force until now be perhaps advisable, especially when one considers that they cannot be observed without sacrifices, sometimes heroic sacrifices?

Or else, by extending to this field the application of the so-called "principle of totality", could one not admit that the intention of a less abundant but more rationally controlled fertility transforms a materially sterilizing intervention into a permissible and wise control of births? Could one not admit, in other words, that the procreative finality pertains to conjugal life considered as a whole, rather than to its single acts? Some also ask whether, in view of modern man's increased sense of responsibility, the moment has not come for him to entrust the objective of birth regulation to his reason and to his will, rather than to the biological rhythms of the human organism.*

Competency of the Magisterium

4. Such questions required from the Church's Magisterium a new and deeper reflection upon the principles of the moral teaching on marriage, a teaching founded on the natural law, illumined and enriched by divine revelation.

None of the faithful will want to deny that the Magisterium of the Church is also competent to interpret the natural moral law. It is, in fact, indisputable, as our predecessors have on numerous occasions declared,[1] that Jesus Christ, when communicating to Peter and to the Apostles His divine authority and sending them to teach His

---

* The Italian text reads "del suo organismo". [Latin: "sui corporis" (of their body).] See nn. 15 & 17.3—TRANS.

[1] See Pius IX, Encyclical *Qui Pluribus*, Nov. 9, 1846: *Pii IX P. M. Acta*, 1, pp. 9–10; St. Pius X, Encyclical *Singulari Quadam*, Sept. 24, 1912: *AAS* 4 (1912), p. 658; Pius XI, Encyclical *Casti Connubii*, Dec. 31, 1930: *AAS* 22 (1930), pp. 579–81; Pius XII, Address to the Episcopate of the Catholic World, Nov. 2, 1954: *AAS* 46 (1954), pp. 671–72; John XXIII, Encyclical *Mater et Magistra*, May 15, 1961: *AAS* 53 (1961), p. 457.

commandments to all nations,[2] constituted them guardians and authentic interpreters of the whole moral law, that is to say, not only of the law of the Gospel, but also of the natural law. For the natural law, too, is an expression of the will of God, and it likewise must be observed faithfully to obtain salvation.[3]

In keeping with this mission of hers, the Church has always provided—and more amply in recent times—a coherent teaching on the nature of marriage as well as on the correct use of conjugal rights and on the duties of husbands and wives.[4]

---

[2] See Mt 28:18–19.

[3] See Mt 7:21.

[4] See *Roman Catechism of the Council of Trent*, Part II, ch. 8; Leo XIII, Encyclical *Arcanum*, Feb. 10, 1880: *Acta Leonis XIII*, 2 (1880), pp. 26–29; *Code of Canon Law*: Canon 1067, Canon 1068, §1; Canon 1076, §§1–2; Pius XI, Encyclical *Divini Illius Magistri*, Dec. 31, 1929: *AAS* 22 (1930), pp. 58–61; Encyclical *Casti Connubii*: *AAS* 22 (1930), pp. 545–46; Pius XII, Address to the Italian Medico-Biological Society of St. Luke, Nov. 12, 1944: *Discorsi e Radiomessaggi di S. S. Pio XII*, 6, pp. 191–92; Address to the Congress of the Italian Catholic Association of Midwives, Oct. 29, 1951: *AAS* 43 (1951), pp. 835–54; Address to the Congress of the Family Front and of the Association of Large Families, Nov. 28, 1951: *AAS* 43 (1951), pp. 857–59; Address to the Seventh Congress of the International Society of Hematology, Sept. 12, 1958: *AAS* 50 (1958), pp. 734–35; John XXIII, Encyclical *Mater et Magistra*: *AAS* 53 (1961), pp. 446–47; Second Vatican Council, Pastoral Constitution *Gaudium*

Special Studies

5. It was precisely from awareness of this mission that we confirmed and enlarged the Study Commission that our predecessor, John XXIII, of venerated memory, had established in March of 1963. This Commission, which included, in addition to numerous experts from the various relevant disciplines, married couples as well, had as its purpose to gather opinions on the new questions concerning married life, and in particular concerning birth regulation, and to furnish useful data so that the Magisterium could give an adequate reply to the expectations not only of the faithful but also of world public opinion.[5]

The labors of these experts, as well as the judgments and counsels later sent to us spontaneously or expressly requested from a good number of our brothers in the episcopate, have permitted

---

et Spes, Dec. 7, 1965, nn. 47–52: *AAS* 58 (1966), pp. 1067–74.

[5] See Paul VI, Address to the Sacred College of Cardinals, June 23, 1964: *AAS* 56 (1964), p. 588; Address to the Commission for the Study of Population, the Family and the Birthrate, March 27, 1965: *AAS* 57 (1965), p. 388; Address to the National Congress of the Italian Society of Obstetrics and Gynecology, Oct. 29, 1966: *AAS* 58 (1966), p. 1168.

us to weigh more accurately all the aspects of this complex matter. Hence, we most sincerely express to all of them our lively gratitude.

Reply of the Magisterium

6. And yet the conclusions reached by the Commission could not be considered by us as final, nor dispense us from a personal examination of the serious question; and this also because, within the Commission itself, no full agreement of judgments concerning the moral norms to be proposed had been reached, and above all because certain criteria for resolving the question had emerged that departed from the moral teaching on marriage proposed with constant firmness by the Magisterium of the Church.

And so, having attentively sifted the documentation offered us, after mature reflection and assiduous prayer, we now intend, by virtue of the mandate entrusted to us by Christ, to give our reply to these grave questions.

II. DOCTRINAL PRINCIPLES

A Total Vision of Man

7. In considering the problem of birth regulation, as is the case for every other problem regarding human life, one must look beyond partial perspectives—whether biological or psychological, demographic or sociological—and make one's consideration in the light of an integral vision of man and of his vocation, not only of his natural and earthly vocation, but also of his supernatural and eternal one. And since, in the attempt to justify artificial methods of birth control, many have appealed either to the demands of conjugal love or to those of "responsible parenthood", it is good to state very precisely the true meaning of these two great realities of married life, recalling principally what was recently set forth in this regard in a highly authoritative form by the Second Vatican Council in the Pastoral Constitution *Gaudium et Spes*.

Conjugal Love

8. Conjugal love reveals its true nature and nobility when it is considered in its supreme

source, God, who is Love,[6] "the Father from whom all fatherhood in heaven and on earth draws its name."[7]

Marriage, therefore, is not the effect of chance or the product of the evolution of blind natural forces; it is a wise institution of the Creator for realizing in mankind His design of love. By means of the reciprocal personal self-giving which is proper and exclusive to them, husband and wife tend to the union of their beings with the goal of helping each other to personal perfection in order to collaborate with God in the begetting and rearing of new lives.

For baptized persons, moreover, marriage takes on the dignity of a sacramental sign of grace, inasmuch as it represents the union of Christ and the Church.

Its Characteristics

9. In this light, one sees clearly the characteristic marks and requirements of conjugal love. It is of the highest importance to have an exact understanding of these marks and requirements.

---

[6] See 1 Jn 4:8.
[7] Eph 3:15.

This love is first of all fully *human*; that is to say, it is at the same time both physical and spiritual. It is not, therefore, a simple transport of instinct and feelings but also, and principally, an act of the free will, destined to endure and to grow by means of the joys and sorrows of daily life, in such a way that husband and wife become one heart and one soul, and together attain their human perfection.

And this love is *total*; that is to say, it is a very special form of personal friendship, in which husband and wife generously share everything, without undue reservations or selfish calculations. Whoever truly loves his spouse, does not love her only for what he receives from her but for herself, happy to be able to enrich her with the gift of himself.

This love is also *faithful* and *exclusive* until death. Such in fact do bride and groom conceive it to be on the day when they freely and with full awareness assume the commitment of the marriage bond. A fidelity such as this can at times be difficult, but that it is always possible, always noble and meritorious, no one can deny. The example of so many married persons down through the centuries shows not only that fidelity is in keeping with the nature of marriage, but that it is also a source of profound and lasting happiness.

Finally, this is a love which is *fruitful* and which is not exhausted by the communion between husband and wife. Rather is it destined to perpetuate itself by bringing new lives into existence. "Marriage and conjugal love are by their nature ordained to the procreation and rearing of children. Indeed, children are the most precious gift of marriage and contribute immensely to the good of the parents themselves."[8]

Responsible Parenthood

10. Hence, conjugal love requires in both husband and wife an awareness of their mission of "responsible parenthood", which today is rightly insisted upon, and which also must be correctly understood. It must be considered under its various legitimate and interrelated aspects.

---

[8] Second Vatican Council, Pastoral Constitution *Gaudium et Spes*, no. 50: *AAS* 58 (1966), pp. 1070–72.

In relation to the biological processes, responsible parenthood means knowing and respecting the functions of these processes; the intellect discovers in the power of giving life biological laws that are part of the human person.[9]

In relation to the tendencies of instinct and of the passions, responsible parenthood means the necessary mastery that reason and will must exercise over them.

In relation to physical, economic, psychological and social conditions, responsible parenthood is exercised either by the well-thought-out and generous decision to raise a large family, or by the decision, made for grave motives* and with respect for the moral law, to avoid a new birth for the time being, or even for an indeterminate period.

Responsible parenthood also and above all implies a more profound relationship to the objective moral order established by God, and of which a right conscience is the faithful interpreter. The responsible exercise of parenthood

---

[9] See St. Thomas, *Summa Theologiae*, I–II, q. 94, art. 2.

* "Gravi motivi". [Latin: "seriis causis" (serious reasons).] See nn. 16.2 & 16.3 (thrice)—TRANS.

implies, therefore, that husband and wife recognize fully their own duties toward God, toward themselves, toward the family and toward society, in a correct hierarchy of values.

In the task of transmitting life, they are not free, therefore, to proceed at will, as if they could determine with complete autonomy the right paths to follow; rather they must conform their actions to the creative intention of God, expressed in the very nature of marriage and of its acts, and manifested by the constant teaching of the Church.[10]

Respect for the Nature and Finality of the Marriage Act

11. These acts, by which husband and wife are united in chaste intimacy and by means of which human life is transmitted, are, as the Council recalled, "good and honorable",[11] and they do not cease to be legitimate if, for causes independent of the will of husband and wife, they

---

[10] See Second Vatican Council, Pastoral Constitution *Gaudium et Spes*, nn. 50–51: *AAS* 58 (1966), pp. 1070–73.
[11] Cf. *ibid.*, no. 49: *AAS* 58 (1966), p. 1070.

are foreseen to be infertile, because they remain ordained to expressing and strengthening their union. Indeed, as experience bears witness, not every act of marital intercourse is followed by a new life. God has wisely arranged natural laws and rhythms of fertility which already of themselves bring about a separation in the succession of births. But the Church, calling men back to the observance of the norms of the natural law, interpreted by her constant teaching, teaches that each and every marriage act must remain open to the transmission of life.* [12]

Two Inseparable Aspects: Union and Procreation

12. This teaching, set forth by the Magisterium on numerous occasions, is founded upon the inseparable connection, willed by God and

---

* "Che qualsiasi atto matrimoniale deve rimanere aperto alla trasmissione della vita". [Latin: "necessarium esse, ut *quilibet matrimonii usus* ad vitam humanam procreandam per se destinatus permaneat" (that *any use whatsoever of marriage* must remain in itself destined to the procreation of human life).] (The italicized words are taken from the Latin of *Casti Connubii*.)—TRANS.

[12] See Pius XI, Encyclical *Casti Connubii*: *AAS* 22 (1930), p. 560; Pius XII, Address to the Congress of the Italian Catholic Association of Midwives: *AAS* 43 (1951), p. 843.

which man may not break on his own initiative, between the two significances of the conjugal act: the unitive significance and the procreative significance.

Indeed, by its intimate structure, the conjugal act, while closely uniting husband and wife, makes them apt for the generation of new lives, according to laws inscribed in the very being of man and woman. By safeguarding both these essential aspects, the unitive and the procreative, the conjugal act preserves in its fullness the sense of true mutual love and its ordination to man's most lofty vocation of parenthood. We think that men of our day are particularly capable of confirming the profoundly reasonable and human character of this fundamental principle.

Faithfulness to God's Design

13. It is, in fact, correctly observed that a conjugal act imposed upon one's spouse without regard for his or her conditions and legitimate desires is not a true act of love, and therefore denies a requirement of the right moral order in

the relations between husband and wife. Hence, one who reflects carefully must also recognize that an act of mutual love that prejudices the capacity to transmit life which God the Creator has inserted therein according to particular laws, is in contradiction with the design constitutive of marriage and with the will of the author of life. Those who make use of this divine gift while destroying, even if only partially, its significance and its finality, act contrary to the nature of both man and woman and of their most intimate relationship, and, therefore, contradict also the plan of God and His will. On the other hand, those who enjoy the gift of conjugal love while respecting the laws of the generative process show that they acknowledge themselves to be not the masters of the sources of human life, but rather the ministers of the design established by the Creator. In fact, just as man does not have unlimited dominion over his body in general, so also, with particular reason, has he no such dominion over his generative faculties as such because of their intrinsic ordination to the bringing into being of life, of which God is the source and origin. "Human life is sacred", John XXIII recalled, "from its very inception it directly involves the creative action of God.''[13]

Unlawful Means of Birth Regulation

14. In conformity with these fundamental elements of the human and Christian vision of marriage, we must once again declare that the direct interruption of the generative process already begun, and, above all, directly willed and procured abortion, even if for therapeutic reasons, are to be absolutely excluded as lawful means of birth regulation.[14]

Also to be excluded, as the Magisterium of the Church has on a number of occasions declared,

---

[13] John XXIII, Encyclical *Mater et Magistra*: *AAS* 53 (1961), p. 447.

[14] See *Roman Catechism of the Council of Trent*, Part II, ch. 8; Pius XI, Encyclical *Casti Connubii*: *AAS* 22 (1930), pp. 562–64; Pius XII, Address to the Italian Medico-Biological Society of St. Luke: *Discorsi e Radiomessaggi di S. S. Pio XII*, 6 (1944), pp. 191–92; Address to the Congress of the Italian Catholic Association of Midwives: *AAS* 43 (1951), pp. 842–43; Address to the Congress of the Family Front and to the Association of Large Families: *AAS* 43 (1951), pp. 857–59; John XXIII, Encyclical *Pacem in Terris*, April 11, 1963: *AAS* 55 (1963), pp. 259–60; Second Vatican Council, Pastoral Constitution *Gaudium et Spes*, n. 51: *AAS* 58 (1966), p. 1072.

is direct sterilization, whether perpetual or temporary, whether of the man or of the woman.[15]

Similarly excluded is every action that, either in anticipation of the conjugal act or in its accomplishment or in the development of its natural consequences, would have as an end or as a means, to render procreation impossible.* [16]

And to justify conjugal acts made intentionally infertile, one cannot invoke as valid reasons the lesser evil, or the fact that when taken together with the fertile acts already performed or to follow later, such acts would coalesce into a whole and hence would share in one and the

---

[15] See Pius XI, Encyclical *Casti Connubii: AAS* 22 (1930), p. 565; Pius XII, Decree of the Holy Office, Feb. 22, 1940: *AAS* 32 (1940), p. 73; Address to the Congress of the Italian Catholic Association of Midwives, *AAS* 43 (1951), pp. 843–44; Address to the Seventh Congress of the International Society of Hematology: *AAS* 50 (1958), pp. 734–35.

* "Di rendere impossibile la procreazione". [Latin: "ut procreatio impediatur" (that procreation be impeded).]—TRANS.

[16] See *Roman Catechism of the Council of Trent*, Part II, ch. 8; Pius XI, Encyclical *Casti Connubii: AAS* 22 (1930), pp. 559–61; Pius XII, Address to the Congress of the Italian Catholic Association of Midwives: *AAS* 43 (1951), p. 843; Address to the Seventh Congress of the International Society of Hematology: *AAS* 50 (1958), pp. 734–35; John XXIII, Encyclical *Mater et Magistra*: *AAS* 53 (1961), p. 447.

same moral goodness. In truth, if it is sometimes permissible to tolerate a lesser moral evil in order to avoid a greater evil or to promote a greater good,[17] it is not permissible, not even for the gravest reasons, to do evil so that good may follow therefrom.[18] One may not, in other words, make into the object of a positive act of the will something that is intrinsically disordered and hence unworthy of the human person, even when the intention is to safeguard or promote individual, family or social goods. Consequently, it is an error to think that a conjugal act which is deliberately made infertile and so is intrinsically wrong could be made right by a fertile conjugal life considered as a whole.

Lawfulness of Therapeutic Means

15. The Church, on the other hand, does not at all consider unlawful the use of those therapeutic means truly necessary to cure diseases of

---

[17] See Pius XII, Address to the Fifth National Congress of the Society of Italian Catholic Jurists, Dec. 6, 1953: *AAS* 45 (1953), pp. 798–99.
[18] See Rom 3:8.

the organism,* even if an impediment to procreation, which may be foreseen, should result
therefrom, provided such an impediment is not,
for whatever motive, directly willed.[19]

Lawfulness of the Recourse to Infertile Times

16. In our day, as we observed above (no. 3),
the objection is made against this teaching of the
Church on conjugal morality that it is the pre-
rogative of human intelligence to master the en-
ergies made available by irrational nature and to
direct them toward an end that is in conformity
with the good of man. Now, some ask, concerning the case at hand, is it not perhaps reasonable in so many circumstances to have recourse
to artificial birth control if thereby are secured
the harmony and tranquility of the family, and
conditions more favorable to the education of

---

* "Dell'organismo". [Latin: "corporis" (of the body).] See
nn. 3.2 & 17.3—TRANS.
[19] See Pius XII, Address to the Twenty-Sixth Congress of
the Italian Association of Urology, Oct. 8, 1953: *AAS* 45
(1953), pp. 674–75; Address to the Seventh Congress of the
International Society of Hematology: *AAS* 50 (1958), pp.
734–35.

children already born? To this question it is necessary to reply with clarity: the Church is the first to praise and recommend the intervention of intelligence in a work that so closely associates the rational creature with his Creator; but she affirms that this must be done with respect for the order established by God.

If, then, there are serious motives* for spacing births, motives deriving from the physical or psychological conditions of husband or wife, or from external circumstances, the Church teaches that it is then permissible to take into account the natural rhythms immanent in the generative functions and to make use of marriage during the infertile times only, and in this way to regulate births without offending the moral principles that we have just recalled.[20]

The Church is consistent when she considers recourse to the infertile times to be permissible, while condemning as always wrong the use of means directly contrary to fertilization, even

---

* "Seri motivi". [Latin: "iustae causae" (proper reasons).] See nn. 10.4 & 16.3 (thrice) — TRANS.

[20] See Pius XII, Address to the Congress of the Italian Catholic Association of Midwives: *AAS* 43 (1951), p. 846.

if such use is inspired by reasons that can appear upright and grave.* In reality, there is an essential difference between the two cases. In the first case, the husband and wife legitimately avail themselves of a natural condition; in the second case, they impede the working of natural processes. It is true that in both cases the husband and wife agree in positively willing to avoid children for acceptable reasons,** seeking to be certain that offspring will not result; but it is likewise true that only in the first case do they prove able to abstain from the use of marriage during the fertile times, when for proper motives*** procreation is not desirable, then making use of it during the infertile times to manifest affection and to safeguard mutual fidelity. By so doing, they give proof of a love that is truly and fully virtuous.

---

* "Ragioni . . . oneste e serie". [Latin: "argumenta . . . honesta et gravia" (arguments . . . upright and grave).] See nn. 10.4 & 16.2 & 16.3 (below, twice)—Trans.

** "Per ragioni plausibili". [Latin: "ob probabiles rationes" (for acceptable reasons).] See nn. 10.4 & 16.2 & 16.3 (above and below)—Trans.

*** "Per giusti motivi". [Latin: "ob iustas rationes" (for proper reasons).] See nn. 10.4 & 16.2 & 16.3 (above, twice) —Trans.

Serious Consequences of Using Artificial Birth Regulation

17. Responsible persons can be still more easily convinced of the solid grounds on which the teaching of the Church in this field is based, if they stop to reflect upon the consequences of the use of the methods of artificial birth regulation. Let them consider, first of all, how wide and easy a road would thus be opened to conjugal infidelity and to a general lowering of morality. One does not need much experience to know human weakness and to understand that human beings—especially the young, who are so vulnerable on this point—have need of encouragement to be faithful to the moral law, and must not be offered an easy means to evade its observance. It can also be feared that the man who becomes used to contraceptive practices, may in the end lose respect for his wife, and no longer caring about her physical and psychological well-being, will come to the point of considering her a mere instrument of selfish enjoyment, and no longer his respected and beloved companion.

Consider also the dangerous weapon that

would thus be placed in the hands of those public authorities who have no concern for the requirements of morality. Who could blame a government for applying, as a solution to the problems of the community, those means acknowledged to be permissible for a married couple in solving a family problem? Who will prevent rulers from favoring, and even imposing upon their people, the method of contraception they judge to be the most effective, if they should consider this to be necessary? In this way, men, while wishing to avoid the individual, family or social difficulties they encounter in observing the divine law, would come to place at the mercy of the intervention of public authorities the most personal and most private sector of conjugal intimacy.

Consequently, if one does not want to see the mission of generating life exposed to the arbitrary decisions of men, one must of necessity recognize certain absolute limits to the possibility of a human being's dominion over his or her body and its functions, limits that no one, whether a private individual or someone invested with authority has any right to exceed. And such limits cannot be determined except by the respect

owed to the integrity of the human organism*
and its functions, according to the principles recalled above and according to the correct understanding of the "principle of totality", explained
by our predecessor, Pius XII.[21]

The Church, Guarantor of Authentic Human Values

18. One can foresee that this teaching will perhaps not be easily received by all: too numerous
are the voices—amplified by today's communications media—which disagree with the voice
of the Church. To tell the truth, it does not sur-
prise the Church that she becomes, like her divine Founder, a "sign of contradiction";[22] yet
she does not, because of this, cease to proclaim
with humble firmness the entire moral law, both

---

* "All'integrità dell'organismo umano". [Latin: "toti hu-
mano corpori" (to the whole human body).] See nn. 3.2 &
15—TRANS.

[21] See Pius XII, Address to the Twenty-Sixth Congress of
the Italian Association of Urology: *AAS* 45 (1953), pp. 674–
75; Address to the Directors and Members of the Italian
Association of Cornea Donors and of the Italian Association
of the Blind, May 14, 1956: *AAS* 48 (1956), pp. 461–62.

[22] Lk 2:34.

the natural law and the law of the Gospel. The Church was not the author of the moral law and therefore cannot be its arbiter; she is only its depository and its interpreter, and can never declare to be permissible that which is not so by reason of its intimate and unchangeable opposition to the true good of man.

In defending conjugal morality in its entirety the Church knows that she contributes to the establishment of a truly human civilization. The Church challenges man not to abandon his own responsibility in exchange for reliance on technical means; by this very fact she defends the dignity of husbands and wives. Faithful to both the teaching and the example of the Savior, she shows herself to be the sincere and disinterested friend of men, whom she wishes to help, even now during their earthly sojourn, "to share as sons in the life of the living God, the Father of all men."[23]

---

[23] Paul VI, Encyclical *Populorum Progressio*, March 26, 1967, n. 21: *AAS* 59 (1967), p. 268.

III. PASTORAL DIRECTIVES

The Church, "Mother and Teacher"

19. Our words would not be an adequate expression of the mind and solicitude of the Church, Mother and Teacher of all peoples, if, after having recalled men to the observance and respect of the divine law regarding matrimony, we did not encourage them in the way of proper birth regulation, even amid the difficult conditions that beset families and peoples today. The Church, in fact, cannot act differently toward men than does the Redeemer: she knows their weakness, has compassion on the multitude, welcomes sinners; but she cannot renounce teaching the law that in reality is proper to human life restored in its original truth and led by the Spirit of God.[24]

Possibility of Observing the Divine Law

20. The teaching of the Church on birth regulation, which is a promulgation of the divine law,

---

[24] See Rom 8.

will easily appear to many to be difficult or even impossible to put into practice. And certainly, like all great and beneficial realities, it calls for serious commitment and many efforts on the part of individuals, of families and of society. Moreover, it would not be livable without the help of God, who supports and strengthens the good will of men. Yet to anyone who weighs the matter well, it must be clear that such efforts ennoble man and benefit the human community.

Mastery of Self

21. A proper practice of birth regulation requires first and foremost that a husband and wife acquire and possess solid convictions about the authentic values of life and of the family, and that they tend to the achievement of perfect self-mastery. To dominate instinct by means of one's reason and free will undoubtedly demands an asceticism in order that the affective expressions of conjugal life be in accord with right order. This is particularly necessary for the observance of periodic continence. Yet this discipline, which is proper to the purity of married couples, far from

harming conjugal love, rather confers upon it a higher human value. It requires continual effort, but thanks to its beneficent influence, husband and wife fully develop their personalities and are enriched with spiritual values. Such discipline bestows upon family life fruits of serenity and peace, and facilitates the solution of other problems; it fosters attention to one's partner, helps both spouses drive out selfishness, the enemy of true love; and it deepens their sense of responsibility. By its means, parents become capable of a deeper and more efficacious influence in the education of their offspring; children and young people grow up with a correct appreciation of human values, and enjoy a serene and harmonious development of their spiritual and emotional faculties.

Creating an Environment Favorable to Chastity

22. On this occasion, we wish to draw the attention of educators and of all those who occupy positions of responsibility for the common good of human society, to the need of creating a climate favorable to the development of

chastity—favorable, that is, to the triumph of healthy liberty over license by means of respect for the moral order. Whatever in the communications media today leads to overstimulation of the senses, to the loosening of morals, as well as every form of pornography and licentious performance, must provoke the open and unanimous reaction of all persons who are deeply concerned about the progress of civilization and the defense of the highest values of the human spirit. It is futile to allege artistic or scientific needs as justification for such depravity,[25] or to deduce an argument in their favor from the freedom allowed in this sector by public authorities.

Appeal to Public Authorities

23. To those who govern in civil society and who are principally responsible for the common good, and can do so much to safeguard morality, we say: Do not allow the morality of your people to be degraded; do not accept that by legal means practices contrary to the natural and divine law

---

[25] See Second Vatican Council, Decree *Inter Mirifica*, nn. 6–7: *AAS* 56 (1964), p. 147.

be introduced into that fundamental cell which is the family. There is another way in which public authorities can and should contribute to the solution of the demographic problem: namely, the way of a provident policy for the family, of a wise educational program that is respectful of the moral law and the liberty of the citizens.

We are well aware of the serious difficulties experienced by public authorities in this regard, especially in developing countries. We devoted our encyclical *Populorum Progressio* to these legitimate concerns of theirs. But with our predecessor, John XXIII, we repeat: "These difficulties are not to be overcome by having recourse to methods and means that are unworthy of man and that are based solely on a purely materialistic concept of man himself and of his life. The true solution is found only in economic development and social progress that respect and promote authentic individual and social human values."[26] And it would be a serious injustice to blame divine providence for what may be due, instead, to insufficient wisdom in government,

---

[26] Encyclical *Mater et Magistra*: *AAS* 53 (1961), p. 447.

to an inadequate sense of social justice, to selfish monopoly, or again to culpable indolence in putting forth the efforts and the sacrifices necessary to ensure a rise in the standard of living for an entire people.[27] Let all responsible public authorities generously redouble their efforts, as some are already laudably doing. And may mutual aid continue to increase among all members of the great human family. This opens up an almost limitless field for the activity of the large international organizations.

To Men of Science

24. We now wish to express our encouragement to men of science, who "can contribute much for the benefit of marriage and the family and for the peace of consciences, if by uniting their efforts they seek to shed more light on the various conditions that make possible a proper regulation of human procreation."[28] It is particularly desirable that, according to the wish ex-

---

[27] See Paul VI, Encyclical *Populorum Progressio*, nn. 48–55: *AAS* 59 (1967), pp. 281–84.

[28] Second Vatican Council, Pastoral Constitution *Gaudium et Spes*, n. 52: *AAS* 58 (1966), p. 1074.

pressed by Pius XII, medical science succeed in
providing a sufficiently secure basis for a regulation of births based on the observation of natural
rhythms.[29] In this way, scientists, and especially
Catholic scientists, will contribute evidence to
demonstrate that, as the Church teaches, "a true
contradiction cannot exist between the divine
laws pertaining to the transmission of life and
those pertaining to the fostering of authentic
conjugal love."[30]

To Christian Husbands and Wives

25. And now we turn our attention more directly to our own sons and daughters, to those
especially whom God calls to serve him in marriage. The Church, while teaching the inviolable
demands of the divine law, announces the tid-
ings of salvation, and by means of the sacraments
opens up the paths of grace, which makes of man
a new creature, capable of corresponding in love

---

[29] See Pius XII, Address to the Congress of the Family Front
and of the Association of Large Families: *AAS* 43 (1951), p.
859.

[30] Second Vatican Council, Pastoral Constitution *Gaudium
et Spes*, n. 51: *AAS* 58 (1966), p. 1072.

and authentic freedom to the design of his Creator and Savior, and of experiencing the gentleness of the yoke of Christ.[31]

Christian married couples, then, docile to the voice of the Church, should recall that their Christian vocation, which began at Baptism, was further specified and reinforced by the sacrament of Matrimony. By means of this sacrament husband and wife are strengthened and, as it were, consecrated for the faithful fulfillment of their specific duties, for the living out of their own vocation unto perfection, and for bearing their own particular Christian witness before the world.[32] To them the Lord entrusts the task of making visible to men the holiness and gentleness of the law that unites the mutual love of husband and wife to their cooperation with the love of God, the Author of human life.

We do not at all intend to hide the sometimes serious difficulties inherent in the life of Christian husbands and wives; for them as for every-

---

[31] See Mt 11:30.

[32] See Second Vatican Council, Pastoral Constitution *Gaudium et Spes*, n. 48: *AAS* 58 (1966), pp. 1067–69; Dogmatic Constitution *Lumen Gentium*, Nov. 21, 1964, n. 35: *AAS* 57 (1965), pp. 40–41.

one else, "the gate is narrow and the way is hard that leads to life."[33] But hope in that life must illumine their way, as with courage they strive to live with wisdom, justice and piety in the present time,[34] knowing that the form of this world passes away.[35]

Let married couples, then, face up to the efforts needed, supported by faith and the hope that "does not disappoint because God's love has been poured out in our hearts through the Holy Spirit, who has been given to us."[36] Let them implore divine assistance by persevering prayer; let them draw grace and charity above all from that inexhaustible font which is the Eucharist. And if sin should still keep its hold over them, let them not be discouraged, but rather let them have recourse with humble perseverance to the mercy of God, which is richly bestowed in the sacrament of Penance. In this way they will be able to achieve the fullness of married life described by the Apostle: "Husbands, love your

---

[33] Mt 7:14; see Heb 12:11.
[34] See Tit 2:12.
[35] See 1 Cor 7:31.
[36] Rom 5:5.

wives as Christ loved the Church. . . . Husbands should love their wives as they do their own bodies. Is not loving one's wife perhaps to love one's self? Now no one has ever hated his own flesh, but rather he nourishes it and cares for it, as Christ does for the Church. . . . This is a great mystery, I mean in reference to Christ and the Church. But in what concerns you, let each one love his wife as himself, and let the wife respect her husband."[37]

Apostolate of Couples

26. Among the fruits that result from a generous effort of fidelity to the divine law, one of the most precious is that married couples themselves not infrequently feel the desire to communicate their experience to others. Thus a new and most noteworthy form of the apostolate of like-to-like comes to be included in the vast field of the vocation of the laity: it is married couples themselves who become apostles and guides to other married couples. Among so many forms

---

[37] Eph 5:25, 28–29, 32–33.

of apostolate, this is assuredly one of those that seem most opportune today.[38]

To Doctors and Medical Personnel

27. We hold in the highest esteem those physicians and medical personnel who, in the exercise of their profession, value above every human interest the higher demands of their Christian vocation. Let them persevere, therefore, in promoting on every occasion the solutions inspired by faith and right reason; and let them strive in their various contacts to convince others and win their respect for these solutions. Let them also consider as their proper professional duty the task of acquiring all the knowledge necessary in this delicate sector, so as to be able to give to the married persons who consult them the wise counsels and sound directives that these have a right to expect.

---

[38] See Second Vatican Council, Dogmatic Constitution *Lumen Gentium*, nn. 35 and 41: *AAS* 57 (1965), pp. 40–41, 45–47; Pastoral Constitution *Gaudium et Spes*, nn. 48–49: *AAS* 58 (1966), pp. 1067–70; Decree *Apostolicam Actuositatem*, Nov. 18, 1965, n. 11: *AAS* 58 (1966), pp. 847–49.

To Priests

28. Beloved sons who are priests: By vocation
you are the counselors and spiritual guides of
individuals and of families. We now turn to you
with confidence. Your first task—especially in
the case of those who teach moral theology—
is to expound without ambiguity the Church's
teaching on marriage. Be the first to give, in
the exercise of your ministry, the example of
loyal internal and external submission to the
Magisterium of the Church. Such submission, as
you well know, obliges not only because of the
reasons given, but much more on account of the
light of the Holy Spirit, which in a particular way
is granted the pastors of the Church to elucidate
the truth.[39] You know, too, that it is of the utmost
importance for the peace of consciences and for
the unity of the Christian people, that in the field
of morals as well as in that of dogma, all should
adhere to the Magisterium of the Church and
should speak the same language. This is why we
most earnestly renew to you the heartfelt plea of

---

[39] See Second Vatican Council, Dogmatic Constitution *Lumen Gentium*, n. 25; *AAS* 57 (1965), pp. 29–31.

the great apostle Paul: "I entreat you, brethren, by the name of Our Lord Jesus Christ, that all of you agree and that there be no divisions among you, but that you be united in the same mind and the same judgment."[40]

29. Not to compromise in any way the saving teaching of Christ is an eminent form of charity for souls. But this must ever be accompanied by patience and goodness, such as the Lord himself gave the example of in dealing with men. Having come not to condemn but to save,[41] he was indeed intransigent with evil, but merciful toward individuals. In their difficulties may married couples always find in the words and in the heart of the priest, the echo of the voice and love of the Redeemer.

And speak with confidence, beloved sons, fully convinced that the Spirit of God, while assisting the Magisterium in proposing doctrine, illumines internally the hearts of the faithful, inviting them to give their assent. Teach married couples the indispensable way of prayer; prepare them to have recourse often and with faith to

---

[40] 1 Cor 1:10.
[41] See Jn 3:17.

the sacraments of the Eucharist and of Penance, without ever allowing themselves to be discouraged by their own weakness.

To Bishops

30. Beloved and venerable brothers in the episcopate, with whom we share more closely in caring for the spiritual good of the people of God: Our respectful and affectionate thoughts turn to you as we conclude this encyclical. To all of you we extend an urgent invitation. Work zealously and incessantly with the priests your collaborators and with your faithful people to safeguard marriage and to keep it holy, so that it may ever be lived more and more in all its human and Christian fullness. Consider this mission one of your most urgent responsibilities at the present time. As you know, this involves concerted pastoral action in all fields of human activity, the economic, the cultural and the social; indeed, only a simultaneous improvement in these various sectors will make it possible to render the life of parents, and of the children within their families, not only tolerable, but easier and

more joyous; to render our common existence in human society more fraternal and peaceful, in faithfulness to God's design for the world.

FINAL APPEAL

31. Venerable brothers, most beloved sons, and all men of good will: Great indeed is the work of education, of progress and of love to which we call you, upon the foundation of the Church's teaching, of which the successor of Peter, together with his brothers in the episcopate, is the depository and interpreter. We are deeply convinced that this is truly a great work, both for the world and for the Church, since man cannot find true happiness, for which he yearns with his whole being, unless he respects the laws inscribed in his nature by God, laws which he ought to observe with understanding and love. Upon this work, and upon all of you, and especially upon married couples, we invoke God's abundant graces of holiness and mercy, and in pledge thereof, we impart to you our apostolic blessing.

Given at Rome, from St. Peter's, on the 25th day of July, the feast of St. James the Apostle, in the year 1968, the sixth of our pontificate.

POPE PAUL VI

A HISTORICAL AFTERWORD

by James Hitchcock

From earliest times the Catholic Church condemned the use of contraceptives, and the Protestant churches retained that prohibition until the 1930 Lambeth Conference of the Anglican Church, which cautiously allowed it. Perhaps partly in response, the next year Pope Pius XI issued the encyclical *Casti Connubii* ("Chaste Marriage"), reaffirming the traditional Christian teaching. But in the following decades virtually all Protestant denominations at least passively accepted artificial birth control, primarily condoms and diaphragms.

The appearance of the first oral contraceptives ("the Pill") in the early 1960s raised expectations that the Catholic Church might reconsider its position. The Second Vatican Council (1962–1965) spoke of the union of the spouses, as one of the purposes of marriage, along with procreation, and this led some people to think that marital union might justify contraception.

At the time much was made of the claim that one of the principal developers of the Pill, Dr. John Rock of Harvard University, was a devout Catholic, as though that in itself might justify use of his invention.

In 1963 Pope John XXIII (1958–1963) established a commission to study questions of birth control and population. Later Pope Paul VI (1963–1978) removed the subject from the floor of the Council and enlarged the commission to fifty-eight members, including married couples. Its authority was consultative only.

The commission held its final meeting in 1966 and made a report to the pope—approved by a majority of its members—advising that the Church should approve at least some forms of contraception for married couples. A minority opposed the report and submitted its own.

Although Paul VI himself reaffirmed the traditional teaching several times in the period 1965–1968, the fact that the question was under study by a commission naturally led to speculation that it would be changed, especially because of the popular impression that the primary purpose of Vatican II was to release Catholics from "outdated" rules and dogmas.

During this crucial period of uncertainty a few Europeans—notably Bishop Wilhelmis Bekkers of the Netherlands and the theologian Louis Janssen of Belgium—openly suggested that the doctrine could and should change. In the United States during that period virtually every significant Catholic journal eventually came to the same conclusion.

As it began to seem likely that the pope would authoritatively pronounce on the subject, some members of the papal commission attempted to force the issue by leaking the majority report to the media. It achieved wide notice and once again seemed to imply that change was inevitable.

Humanae Vitae was issued on July 25, 1968. The year was crucial in terms of the negative reaction to the encyclical, because it was the peak year of a world-wide rebellion against authority that had been building up for half a decade and that manifested itself in politics, education, religion, and many other things. The rejection of all sexual restraints was at the heart of this "counter culture", and *Humanae Vitae* was a direct challenge to that rebellion.

While the culture at large greeted the encyclical with extreme hostility, there was often virulent dissent within the Church as well, with assertions that it was "incompatible with the new climate of growth and responsibility in the Church", "difficult if not impossible for married couples", and "the pope has defaulted on his real role, which is to communicate the challenge of the Gospel to the contemporary world."

Within a day of the encyclical's having been issued, the moral theologian Charles Curran composed a statement that concluded that "spouses may responsibly decide according to their conscience that artificial contraception in some circumstances is permissible and indeed necessary to preserve and foster the value and sacredness of marriage."

The statement was eventually signed by over 600 people, mainly priests. Among the more notable signers were: the moral theologians J. Giles Milhaven, Daniel Maguire, and Charles Curran; the dogmatic theologians Walter Burghardt, Richard McBrien, and David Tracy; the Scripture scholars Roland Murphy, Dominic Crossan, and Joseph Clifford; the catechetical theologians Berard Marthaler, Alfred McBride, and Gabriel Moran; the liturgists Godfrey Diekmann and Aidan Kavanaugh; the lay charismatic leader Kevin Ranaghan; the sociologist Joseph Fichter; and the anti-war activist Gordon Zahn.

One signer, John A. O'Brien, was an elderly priest who at one time had been a leading Catholic apologist but who had become a severe critic of the contraception doctrine. Another was a Boston priest, Paul Shanley, who would later go to prison as one of the most egregious of the clerical sexual molesters.

Celibate priests had no personal stake in the practice of contraception, and for many the real issue was Church discipline. They had expected that there would be an end to mandatory celibacy, and soon priests and religious began abandoning their vocations in large numbers.

For many Catholics *Humanae Vitae* was embarrassing evidence that the Church had failed to update itself. Cardinal Leo Joseph Suenens of Belgium, who had been a leading figure at the Council, questioned "whether moral theology took sufficient account of scientific progress, which can help determine what is according to nature. I beg you my brothers let us avoid another Galileo affair. One is enough."

But for Suenens and many others the real issue was the locus of authority in the Church. He criticized the pope's decision for having frustrated the collegiality that had been defined by the Council, and theologians started claiming to be a "second magisterium" whose authority had weight equal to that of the hierarchy.

There was a good deal of personal ego involved—John Rock left the Church when the Pill was not approved, and Mrs. Patrick Crowley, a member of the papal commission, said, "I have never forgiven the Church for *Humanae Vitae.*"

The Curran statement gave the idea of conscience a meaning it had never previously had in Catholic theology but that fit with the morally permissive atmosphere of the 1960s. The theologian Avery Dulles (later a cardinal) said that using the encyclical as a test of Catholic orthodoxy was contrary to "the American tradition of freedom and pluralism . . . the spirit of personal responsibility, which has done so much to invigorate American Catholicism in the past few years."

The influential *Dutch Catechism* of 1966 invoked the idea of the development of doctrine to justify a change in the teaching and said that the Council did not exclude any method of contraception.

Virtually all Protestant leaders criticized the encyclical, but the Orthodox patriarch Athenagoras supported it.

The publication of the encyclical was followed by open dissent by the laity, but for a time the dissent continued to be led by clergy. Lay people who denied that the pope had the authority to forbid contraception sometimes illogically justified its practice by appeals to the authority of particular priests.

Years later the English Bishop Christopher Butler stated that the encyclical had not been "received" by the church and was thus "invalid". (Years later still, Avery Dulles, as cardinal, took issue with this argument, noting that mere non-acceptance does not count as evidence against the truth of a teaching. He warned that the Church must be on guard against the spirit of the age and referred to the task of the Magisterium to bear witness "in season and out of season", a rather different stance than he took in 1968.)

The bishops of Canada, in an official statement, in effect said that contraception use was a matter of conscience, and the Belgian bishops pronounced that someone who is "capable of forming a personal and well-founded judgment . . . has the right to follow his conviction provided that he remains sincerely disposed to continue his inquiry".

The bishops of the United States said that dissent was permissible "only if the reasons are serious and well founded, if the manner of the dissent does not question or impugn the teaching authority of the Church and is such as not to give scandal", conditions that were rarely taken seriously.

The stipulation that Catholics had to make an honest effort to accept the directives of the encyclical was largely ignored in an atmosphere of overwhelming hostility to the teaching, which theologians and even bishops often implied was in error.

Although at Vatican II the Church had ostensibly manifested its world-wide character, the discussion of *Humanae Vitae* took place largely within the context of Western Europe and North America.

Little noticed in that debate was the fact that in Latin America there was much support for the encyclical, because of resentment of the fact that various international agencies, such as the World Bank, were pressuring poorer countries to introduce birth control. (Years after the Pill had been marketed it was revealed that Rock and others had conducted tests on poor women in Puerto Rico without warning them of side effects and that several died during the trials.)

Paul VI sometimes reaffirmed the teachings of *Humanae Vitae*, but he was troubled by the reactions it provoked and the impression grew that it was to be regarded as a theoretical statement only. Many people assumed it was a dead letter.

When Cardinal Patrick A. O'Boyle of Washington suspended a number of priests who publicly dissented from the encyclical, they appealed to the Holy See, which ordered them reinstated. O'Boyle's attempt to dismiss Curran from the faculty of the Catholic University of America failed when he could not get the full support of the bishops on the university board.

But the teaching survived and even gained greater credibility.

As patriarch of Venice, John Paul I (1978) supported *Humanae Vitae*.

As Cardinal Karol Wojtyła of Krakow, Pope John Paul II (1978–2005) had some influence on the substance of the encyclical, and from the beginning of his pontificate he repeatedly invoked it and insisted that it was not "open to free discussion among theologians", something that would "lead the moral consciences of spouses into error". Once again there were protests, especially from Germany.

The Synod of Bishops of 1980 was devoted to the family. Archbishop John R. Quinn of San Francisco noted the widespread doubts about *Humanae Vitae* and cited the principle of doctrinal development, proposing that the entire subject be reopened for a world-wide dialogue.

In his 1993 encyclical *Veritatis Splendor* ("the splendor of truth") John Paul addressed the subject of conscience in arriving at moral decisions: "The authority which the magisterium enjoys by the will of Christ exists so that the moral conscience can attain the truth with security and remain in it."

John Paul raised the entire subject to a higher theological level, delivering over a hundred addresses relating to marital love that coalesced as the "Theology of the Body". In his apostolic exhortation *Familiaris Consortio* ("the community of the Family") (1981), he spoke of marital love in personalistic terms—"the total reciprocal self-giving of husband and wife", whereas contraception involves "not giving oneself totally to the other".

The *Catechism of the Catholic Church*, promulgated by Pope John Paul II in 1992, declared contraceptive acts intrinsically evil and incorporated not only the language of *Humanae Vitae* but also the teaching of *Familiaris Consortio*. Of lesser significance, but still noteworthy, is the Holy See's 1997 *Vademecum for Confessors*, which dealt with the intrinsic evil of contraception and which provided guidance for pastors on the subject.

Pope Benedict XVI (2005–2013) called *Humanae Vitae* "a sign of contradiction but also of continuity of the Church's doctrine and tradition". Following the personalist theology of John Paul II, he warned that if the unity of soul and body is broken—if only the body is satisfied —love becomes a "commodity".

While Paul VI did not use the familiar phrase "slippery slope", he foresaw the far-reaching effects of contraception.

At the time of the Council, Catholics who urged that birth control be legitimized held a very circumspect position—it would be allowed only to give married couples a measure of control over the size of their families and the spacing of pregnancies, but it would not be used in order to remain completely childless. Under no circumstances was it to be used outside marriage.

The initial claim that objections to mechanical contraceptives did not apply to the Pill was soon seen to be specious.

The radical implications of separating sexual intercourse from procreation were of necessity minimized at first, but amidst the fevered atmosphere of the sexual revolution of the late 1960s all restraints were quickly discarded. Many liberal Catholics, notably Charles Curran, eventually justified virtually every phase of that revolution, as it unfolded step by step.

Some people did not feel suited to be parents,

or at least did not wish to assume that responsibility. Why could they not enjoy marital love without fear of pregnancy?

If sexual intercourse was the highest expression of love between two people, why could it not be enjoyed by those who were planning to marry as well as by married couples?

Two people might love one another but were not able or did not wish to marry. For them also the loving union of sexual intercourse was legitimate.

But why was intercourse necessarily linked to love? The new atmosphere of liberation recognized that pleasure itself was valid. Fear of pregnancy was the only objection to "recreational sex".

Dissenters from *Humanae Vitae* argued that contraception would preclude the need for abortion, and the Church was strongly criticized for its failure to recognize that fact. But, as could have been expected, history showed otherwise —the incidence of abortion rose astronomically, along with the ubiquitous availability of contraceptives. If there is a right to have intercourse without pregnancy, abortion is the natural next step when contraception fails. (Some Catholics do remain opposed to abortion while accepting contraception.)

Homosexuality is the most recent stage of the sexual revolution (polygamy is still to come). Homosexuality was held in abeyance for a time even though logic justified it, once sex and procreation had been sundered. The homosexual revolution concentrated on "marriage" but, as with heterosexuals, the prevailing view of sex does not require the partners to be committed to one another.

Paul VI warned that marital fidelity would be threatened by the contraceptive mentality, and divorce rates have skyrocketed even faster than abortions. With the personal fulfillment of the spouses now taken as the primary purpose of marriage, any diminution of that experience can easily lead to renewed searching outside marriage, with the welfare of children a secondary consideration.

Long before China instituted her "one child" policy, Paul VI also feared that the widespread acceptance of contraception would allow governments to impose it on their people.

Although most Catholics dissent from Church teaching on contraception (or are unaware of it), under John Paul II and Benedict XVI there was a modest resurgence of support, partly because he tended to appoint bishops committed to the teaching. There have also been substantial improvements in the methods of natural family planning. Perhaps significantly, many of the scholars and popular speakers engaged in explicating the encyclical are lay people. These include Janet Smith, Mary Eberstadt, Germain Grisez, William E. May, Mary Healy, Jason and Crystalina Evert, Scott and Kimberly Hahn, Christopher West, Edward Sri, Teresa Tomeo, John and Sheila Kippley, Matt Fradd, Angela Franks, and Patrick Coffin. There also have been some stirrings of interest by Evangelical Protestants.

POSTSCRIPT

We're Finally Ready for *Humanae Vitae*

by Jennifer Fulwiler

I sat in the pew at Mass on a recent Sunday, listening to our associate pastor, Father Jonathan Raia, give a homily about a new crop of threats to religious freedom. As usual, the parishioners listened with varying levels of attentiveness, most of us slouched in casual posture, some people glancing around the room, others distracted by young children. But then Father said something that caused the feeling in the room to change. He made a passing allusion to the fact that the Catholic Church is opposed to contraception, and instantly a tension rippled through the pews. People sat up. Some leaned forward to hear better. The wandering gazes were now locked onto our young priest.

This most controversial of Catholic teachings

had been splashed all over the news in recent months, ridiculed and denounced throughout popular culture. It was the issue that Catholics whispered about behind closed doors, but that was almost never addressed openly at the parish level. The question hung in the air:

"Is he going to go there?"

He did.

In the second half of his homily, Father Jonathan gently but unflinchingly explained that the Catholic Church teaches that contraception is bad. He teased out the reasoning behind this doctrine, articulated why child spacing by natural methods is different than child spacing by contraception, and pointed people to resources where they could discover reliable methods of Natural Family Planning. As he spoke, the thought came to mind:

I think we're finally ready for this.

In the almost ten years that I have been going to Catholic churches, I have never heard a priest speak so directly about the Church's teaching in this area—and I can understand why. For decades our culture has perceived contraception as being akin to air or water: a categorically good and absolutely necessary resource. Only an institution with the most nefarious motives would object to all people incorporating this invaluable blessing into their lives, the thinking went. Undoubtedly, many priests have avoided the subject in their homilies because they knew that the misunderstanding on this topic was so deep and so widespread that they would need hours of speaking time even to begin to address it properly.

But things are changing now. Just as the tide is turning on the issue of abortion (a recent Gallup poll showing that fifty-three percent of Americans under age thirty-five believe that abortion is morally wrong), I believe it is turning with contraception too. More and more couples are realizing that contraception does not make marriage easier; Catholic couples who have struggled to use Natural Family Planning are seeing that contraception is not a solution, but in fact brings in a whole host of new challenges.

After forty years of widespread access to artificial birth control, it is dawning on people that contraception has not been the cure-all it was supposed to be. Statistics from the Guttmacher Institute show that over half of women seeking abortions were using contraception at the time they conceived, and an entire generation of Americans has had this backed up by personal experience. The gleeful message that the Pill will lead to women's freedom might have worked in the 1960s, but it falls flat in an era when too many people know a woman who ended up sitting in an abortion doctor's waiting room after her contraception failed her. The tension is building as more and more men and women are disappointed by the "solution" of contraception, and the time is ripe for the message that there's another way.

As we sat listening to Father Jonathan's homily that Sunday, I think we were all surprised to hear such an open discussion of this topic. Not only did he directly state the Church's teaching, but he gently challenged those who do not currently accept this doctrine to reconsider their stance. In the tone of a caring father, he suggested that each of us pray for our own conversion on the issue of respect for life and human sexuality, wherever we may be in need of it.

He concluded by saying: "This is at the heart of our Faith, because it's at the heart of who we are as human beings."

When he finished, the church was still. The topic had been hotly debated all over the country in recent days, and there was an electric silence as we internalized what he said. We also wondered how our fellow parishioners would react. There had been so much media speculation about Catholics' opinions on this issue, most of it claiming that the average man or woman in the pew is hostile to this area of the Church's teaching. How would the thousand-plus people here in this room receive this homily?

As Father Jonathan returned to his chair at the side of the altar, the question was suddenly answered. The pews erupted in spontaneous, thunderous applause.

FOR FURTHER READING

Budziszewski, J. *On the Meaning of Sex*. Wilmington, Del.: Intercollegiate Studies Institute, 2012.

Coffin, Patrick. *Sex au Naturel: What It Is and Why It's Good for Your Marriage*. Steubenville, Ohio: Emmaus Road Publishing, 2010.

Eberstadt, Mary. *Adam and Eve after the Pill: The Paradoxes of the Sexual Revolution*. San Francisco: Ignatius Press, 2012.

Franks, Angelica. *Contraception and Catholicism: What the Church Teaches and Why*. Boston: Pauline Books & Media, 2013.

Healy, Mary. *Men and Women Are from Eden: A Study Guide to John Paul II's Theology of the Body*. Cincinnati: Servant Books, 2005.

Hogan, Robert and John M. LeVoir. *Covenant of Love: Pope John Paul II on Sexuality, Marriage,* and Family in the Modern World. San Francisco: Ignatius Press, 1992.

John Paul II. *Man and Woman He Created Them: A Theology of the Body*. Boston: Pauline Books & Media, 2006.

Kaczor, Christopher and Jennifer Kaczor. *The Seven Big Myths about Marriage: Wisdom from Faith, Philosophy, and Science about Happiness and Love*. San Francisco: Ignatius Press, 2014.

Kippley, John. *Sex and the Marriage Covenant: A Basis for Morality*. San Francisco: Ignatius Press, 2005.

May, William E. *Marriage: The Rock on Which the Family Is Built*, 2nd ed. San Francisco: Ignatius Press, 2009.

———. *Theology of the Body in Context: Genesis and Growth*. Boston: Pauline Books & Media, 2010.

Medina-Estevez, Jorge Cardinal. *Male and Female He Created Them: Essays on Marriage and the Family*. San Francisco: Ignatius Press, 2004.

Smith, Janet E. *Humanae Vitae, a Generation Later.* Washington, D.C.: Catholic University of America Press, 1991.

———. *Why Humanae Vitae Was Right.* San Francisco: Ignatius Press, 1993.

Sri, Edward. *Men, Women and the Mystery of Love: Practical Insights from John Paul II's Love and Responsibility.* Cincinnati: Servant Books, 2007.

Tomeo, Teresa. *Extreme Makeover: Women Transformed by Christ, Not Conformed to the Culture.* San Francisco: Ignatius Press, 2011.

Wojtyła, Karol. *Love and Responsibility.* San Francisco: Ignatius Press, 1993.